- Inside Special Operations™ -

USMC RECONNAISSANCE BATTALIONS

Tamra B. Orr

Warrenville Public
Library District
28W751 Stafford Place
Warrenville, IL 60555

Published in 2009 by The Rosen Publishing Group, Inc.
29 East 21st Street, New York, NY 10010

First Edition

Library of Congress Cataloging-in-Publication Data

Orr, Tamra.
USMC reconnaissance battalions / Tamra B. Orr.
    p. cm.—(Inside Special Operations)
Includes bibliographical references.
ISBN-13: 978-1-4042-1846-8 (lib. bdg.)
ISBN-13: 978-1-4358-5132-0 (pbk.)
6-pack ISBN-13: 978-1-4042-7863-9

1. United States. Marine Corps—Commando troops. 2. United States. Marine Corps. Force Reconnaissance Company, 1st. I. Title. II. Title: United States Marine Corps reconnaissance battalions.
VE23.O74 2008
359.9'631—dc22

                                                                2008006966

Manufactured in Malaysia

On the cover: Sergeant Boyce of the 3rd Reconnaissance Battalion, 3rd Marine Division, takes careful aim during training at the Shoalwater Bay Training Area in 2003.

Ollis Book Corp. 10/14/09 $21.95

Contents

Here, the 3rd Marine Reconnaissance Battalion quietly heads to the "shoot house," a rubber-encased structure where they learn all about explosives and other weaponry.

Introduction:

The Few. The Proud. The Marines.

It is a familiar motto: "The Few. The Proud. The Marines." It's heard on television commercials, at recruitment meetings, and even on the nightly news. However, the U.S. Marines have existed since 1775, and their official motto is *Semper Fidelis*, a Latin phrase meaning "Always Faithful." The second smallest of the five branches of the armed forces, the U.S. Marine Corps has approximately 180,000 active-duty members. These men and women share their mission, their jobs, and their dedication. Time-honored traditions—from the serious to the silly—are passed from one generation to the next. As Aulton Kohn, a Parris Island Museum information receptionist, states in an article on the Marine Corps Web site, "It is the tradition, the history that makes the Marines stand out. The stories passed from drill instructor to recruit and from Marine to Marine, they add the color to the Corps."

The core values of honor, courage, and commitment are extremely important to the U.S. Marines, especially to the smaller division of the Recon Marines. On the Marine Corps Web site, under the quality of honor, it says members of the Marine Corps will conduct themselves ethically in all of their relationships, as well as maintain high levels of honesty and truthfulness. It is stated that they will "encourage new ideas and deliver the bad news, even when it is unpopular," as well as follow a strict code that involves integrity, responsibility, and reliability. They promise to follow their legal and ethical responsibilities both publicly and personally at all times. The code states that "illegal or improper behavior or even the appearance of such behavior will not be tolerated." They place a high priority on being accountable for everything they say and do and on being "mindful of the privilege to serve [their] fellow Americans."

Another important part of the U.S. Marine code is courage. Recon Marines swear to support and defend and to have the "courage to meet the demand of [their] profession and the mission when it is hazardous, demanding or otherwise difficult." They take this oath seriously, promising to defend the nation regardless of personal consequences. As the code is phrased, "Courage is the value that gives us the moral and mental strength to do what is right, even in the face of personal or professional adversity."

Along with honesty and courage, another high priority for the Recon Marines is commitment. The emphasis on obeying orders and following the chain of command is necessary in the armed forces. This part of the code also includes respect for all people without regard to race, religion, or gender. Moral character, technical excellence, and working together as a team are integral parts of the force.

As brave and dedicated as all marines are expected to be, there is a special faction of them that faces even greater expectations. They are expected to work harder, take more risks, learn more skills, and serve their country with even greater dedication, earning them the respect of officers and civilians alike. These men make up the USMC's Reconnaissance Battalions.

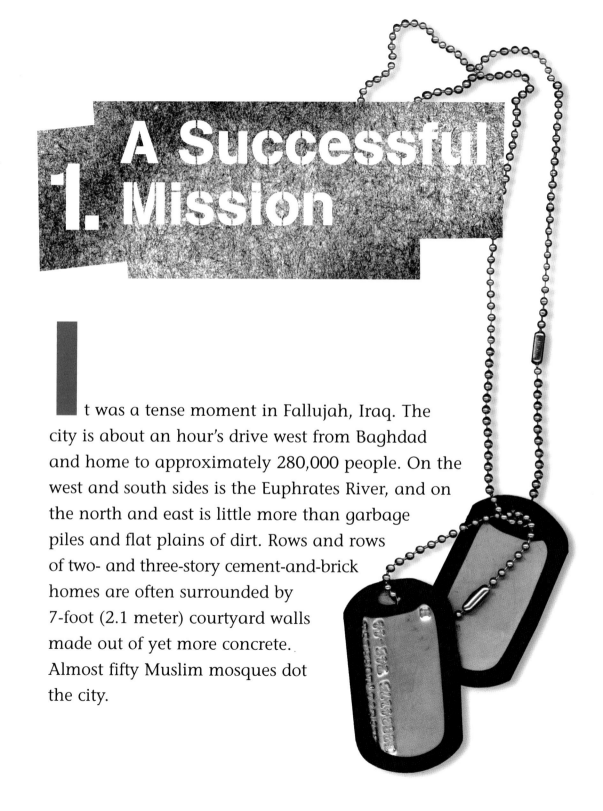

1. A Successful Mission

It was a tense moment in Fallujah, Iraq. The city is about an hour's drive west from Baghdad and home to approximately 280,000 people. On the west and south sides is the Euphrates River, and on the north and east is little more than garbage piles and flat plains of dirt. Rows and rows of two- and three-story cement-and-brick homes are often surrounded by 7-foot (2.1 meter) courtyard walls made out of yet more concrete. Almost fifty Muslim mosques dot the city.

Clearing and searching houses is one of the main tasks that Recon Marines learn to do. It is often a risky process and, therefore, requires a great deal of caution—and courage.

The 1st Reconnaissance Battalion, Regimental Combat Team 6, had been sent to Fallujah in October 2007 to put a stop to the repeated roadside bombings that had killed or injured many soldiers and destroyed a number of vehicles. The team had been waiting all day for the signal to go ahead and investigate, and they had been watching for any odd or suspicious activity on the roadways that had been targeted by the terrorists.

Finally, as dark descended, Sergeant Kenneth D. Russell and his team got the message to go in. "We got intelligence from talking to other people in the area, and the area we ended up going to was a bad place," Russell says in an article posted on

Military.com. "[Insurgents] were driving back and forth. We took the intelligence and ended up moving further into the area and within an hour of being there, [bad things] started happening."

First, the team encountered an empty house. Two members of the unit—the radio operator and the squad automatic weapon gunner—searched the house. Something was wrong. It was just too quiet, too empty. Even odder, there was livestock roaming aimlessly around the property.

"People don't normally leave their farm animals behind, so we got a real funny feeling about it," explains Russell. The team holed up in the house, and two men went up to the roof to secure it. Russell and another marine began searching other nearby houses for a place to set up their surveillance.

The team had just reunited when Sergeant Alexander MacDonald spotted something unusual: a wire that led out into the home's courtyard. Where was it going? He followed it with his eyes and saw that it went through the courtyard, across the road to the opposite side, and finally into a reed-filled ditch. This looked exactly like the site of a roadside bomb.

Carefully, the men traced the wire and found a huge hole dug into the ground. It was so big, an entire car could fit into it. Without saying a word, the team knew what was going on. "We don't have to say anything to one another," Russell says.

Above, a marine is knocked to the ground by an improvised explosive device in Anah, Iraq. A number of marines spent almost three months in Rawah and Anah (northwest of Baghdad), learning about security operations.

"We just kind of know what each one of us is thinking." The wire was cut, and the men went back to the house to wait, hoping to catch terrorists in the act of setting another bomb.

Ninety minutes passed. Finally, through their night-vision goggles, the men spotted activity along the tree line. Two men were approaching, toting weapons, wire, and other material. It was clear to the recon team that these men intended to set and eventually detonate a bomb. "Hostile intent" thus confirmed, it was time to take action.

MacDonald picked up his sniper rifle. So did Russell. Together, the two marines zeroed in on their target. When the shot was perfect and the timing was right, the enemy was eliminated.

For doing their job well and efficiently, members of the unit were praised by their commander, Colonel Richard Simcock. "It without a doubt saves Marines' lives with those two [insurgents] gone," he says in the article on Military.com. "It's guaranteed that those two will never hurt another Marine, that's a key thing. This is mission accomplishment for those guys."

It was a typical mission for the Recon Marines.

2. A History Lesson

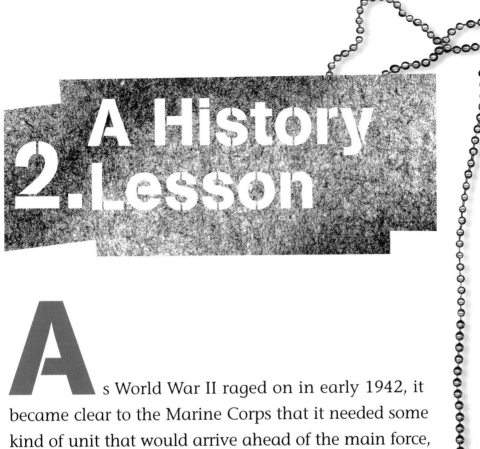

As World War II raged on in early 1942, it became clear to the Marine Corps that it needed some kind of unit that would arrive ahead of the main force, providing top-secret, essential information. The Raider Battalions were formed to do just that. Another group, the Observation Group of the 1st Marine Division, was also formed for that purpose. The Observation Group began with only two officers and twenty enlisted men. By 1943, it had expanded to ninety-eight marines, and the name had been

Knowing how to get in and out of a helicopter quickly has always been essential to Recon Marines. Here, the 1st Marine Division Reconnaissance Company invades Hill 812 in Korea on September 20, 1951.

changed to the Amphibious Recon Company. In one of their first covert missions, they were delivered by submarine to the Pacific island of Apamama to survey the island and report back. Although they were shot at, they set up a fortress and cleared the way for the other marines to invade.

The Marine Corps was pleased. This new group had been amazingly effective; it was time to expand again. Two officers, 270 enlisted men, and thirteen navy doctors then made up the team. They took part in landings at Tinian Island, Iwo Jima, and Okinawa. When World War II came to an end, however, the units did not end with it.

The reconnaissance group became active once again in the Korean War (1950–1953), this time by the name of the Amphibious Recon Platoon. The group was sent into North Korea to make reports as well as raid rail lines and tunnels. Some of these missions were 40 miles (64 kilometers) past enemy lines.

Once the Korean War was over, the Marine Corps decided it was time for some restructuring and updating. Members of the platoon were sent to a variety of training schools to learn more about parachute jumping, diving, and boat skills. Finally, in 1957, the 1st Force Reconnaissance Company was created. The second followed in June 1958.

Into Vietnam

The need for these recon groups became even clearer during the Vietnam War (1959–1975). The Marine Corps quickly realized that it needed more in-depth information on enemy forces. It wanted to know the Vietnamese's strengths, weaknesses, habits, and customs. To do this, it needed small teams that could watch the enemy for days in a row. It needed men who could set up ambushes and take prisoners for interrogating. The recon units were perfect for the job. Because they were small units and not based near the other troops, they could sneak in more easily and usually avoid being caught or joined in battle.

Of course, being so close to the enemy for days at a time entailed a great deal of risk for these men. If they were spotted, it would not take long to surround and overwhelm them. To give them more protection, air and artillery support was always waiting for their distress call. If the recon team was

Getting down and dirty is all part of the routine for recon platoons. In this photo, troops search for Viet Cong hideouts in the thick jungles of Saigon, South Vietnam, in 1965.

discovered, the members knew the procedure: pump out as much weapon fire as they were capable of to keep the Vietnamese back—just long enough for support to catch up, cover them, and get them out of the area.

Today's Global War on Terror

Recon Marines play a vital part in today's war against terrorists, although their roles in this battle are not the same as in the past. There are no front lines to penetrate. Most of their patrolling is done in Humvees rather than on foot. They are typically dressed in Kevlar helmets and body armor and gather their intelligence in face-to-face situations rather than from afar. Also, instead of just getting data and then passing it on to higher command (as they have done in the past), the recon groups are able to act on the data and make independent decisions about what actions to take, including using their weapons. "It used to be in reconnaissance, if you fired a shot, you failed your mission," says Gunnery Sergeant Kenneth A. Westgate in an article on the Marine Corps News Web site. "Now, we're expected to make contact. It's not that we've lost a mission. We've gained more mission. We're collecting, analyzing and prosecuting almost all at the platoon level. The mission we're tasked with now is different." Westgate points out that not only have some of the duties changed, but so has the equipment. "When I first started it was boonie covers [hats] and heavy rucks. Now it's Humvees and heavy machine guns," he says. "The pace of warfare has changed."

Marines such as Sgt. Joshua S. Adams are incredibly grateful for their small-arms protective inserts. Wearing his is what saved Adams's life when he was shot in the chest by a sniper in Habbaniya, Iraq.

Current Marine Reconnaissance Battalions

1st Reconnaissance Battalion: 1st Marine Division (stand-alone)

2nd Reconnaissance Battalion: 2nd Marine Division (East Coast)

3rd Reconnaissance Battalion: 3rd Marine Division (Okinawa)

4th Reconnaissance Battalion: Reserves (Alabama and Hawaii)

The role of Recon Marines in Iraq is much more up close and personal than it was in previous conflicts. Instead of watching through binoculars from a distance, men are walking through the villages, talking with the people in order to get information. As Gunnery Sgt. Mark Oliva phrases it on the Marine Corps News Web site, "Recon Marines are part beat cop, keeping the peace. They're part investigator, putting together the puzzle and part SWAT, kicking down the door to snatch the bad guys." Although adjusting to changes has been harder for the more seasoned marines, they also see some distinct advantages to it.

"We have much more supply with us on the humvees instead of what we used to carry in our rucks," Westgate says in the Marine Corps News Web site article. "We can move longer distances quicker . . . What we've done is put another tool in our toolbox, but we've also put another mission in our pack."

In September 2006, a group of Recon Marines hit the streets of Fallujah, Iraq, armed with a different kind of equipment: bolt cutters and sledgehammers. In Operation Matador, the 2nd Reconnaissance Battalion was assigned to search hundreds of stores and dozens of buildings throughout Fallujah. Working alongside Iraqi army soldiers, Iraqi police, and additional U.S. Marine regiments, the Recon Marines made their way through the city, cutting locks. In the September 13, 2006, edition of the Marine Corps News Web site, Sergeant Jason Salvog states, "We had to have broken more than 200 locks today. Some of the doors we got through had five locks on them. We dulled our bolt cutters."

Building by building, lock by lock, the battalion made its way through the eerily silent city. The quiet was broken, however, when the sledgehammers came into play. "Working in an urban environment is really different than some of the other things we do," explains Corporal Lynn Westover Jr. in the September 13, 2006, edition of the Marine Corps News Web site. "There are so many places people could be. They live here. They know every room. It's like going to your own hometown where you grew up. You just know all the areas."

Working with Iraqis themselves was also challenging. "The toughest part is the language barriers," adds Salvog. "We also have to keep in mind that they're not Marines. They're working at a different standard."

Meet the "Highlanders"

The 1st Light Armored Vehicle Battalion, also known as the "Highlanders" was activated in 1985. In 1990, it was deployed to southwest Asia when Iraq invaded Kuwait in the First Gulf War. It did reconnaissance at the Kuwait–Saudi Arabian border and destroyed a number of enemy forces. It was one of the very first battalions to enter Kuwait City, and it captured the city's international airport.

Like most of the armed forces, the Highlanders were deployed to Iraq for Operation Iraqi Freedom in 2003. They played an important role in securing the capital, Baghdad. They also assisted in Task Force Tripoli when they advanced and took Tikrit, the hometown of Saddam Hussein. The Highlanders then returned to Iraq a year later and helped patrol the western borders of Iraq to prevent weapons and soldiers from crossing.

Some of the missions that Recon Marines are sent on, of course, are within U.S. borders. For example, in May 1992,

Much of a marine's time is made up of practicing for future combat. Here, the 3rd Battalion's 1st Marine Division practices squad rushes in northern Kuwait.

the Highlanders were sent to Los Angeles, California, to help the Long Beach Police Department cope with the riots and looting that followed the Rodney King trial.

Meet the "Iron Horse Marines"

The 4th Light Armored Reconnaissance Battalion was first activated in 1987. It, too, was sent to Saudi Arabia as part of Operation Desert Shield and Operation Desert Storm during the First Gulf War, from the end of 1990 to spring 1991. Marines were scattered out across hundreds of miles of Iraqi desert.

Helping Civil Disturbances

In May 1992, the city of Los Angeles erupted in racial tension and anger when four police officers were acquitted after being brought up on charges for beating a black motorist named Rodney King. After a high-speed car chase, the officers stopped King and then, stating that he had resisted arrest, beat him. The beating was caught on videotape. When the officers were found innocent, it sparked citywide riots involving looting, assaults, arson, and murder. By the time it ended, fifty-three people had died.

Rodney King

While they were there, they rescued friendly forces, crossed minefields, and captured prisoners. They were nicknamed the "Iron Horse Marines."

This team was called upon once again during the Second Gulf War in 2003 to help with Operation Iraqi Freedom. The team was deployed along the Iraq–Iran border. Members conducted a number of raids while there and were given the Presidential Unit Citation for their work. Since then, additional Recon Marines have been involved in the global war on terror.

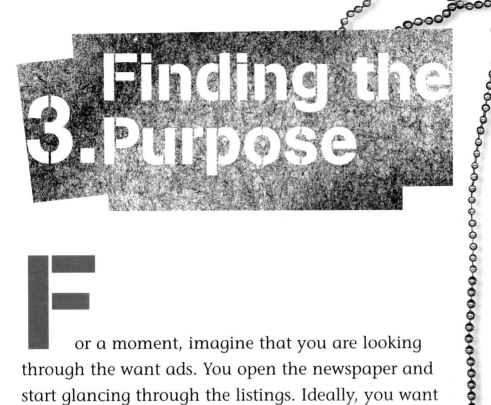

3. Finding the Purpose

For a moment, imagine that you are looking through the want ads. You open the newspaper and start glancing through the listings. Ideally, you want a challenging job that will push your boundaries. You want some adventure, some excitement. Suppose you came across an ad that read like this:

Looking for someone who knows basic infantry skills. Must also possess advanced proficiency in swimming, small-boat operations, close-combat skills, helicopter and submarine insertion and extraction techniques, assault climbing, demolitions, communications, photography, threat weapons and equipment, and initial terminal guidance operations for heliborne, airborne, and waterborne forces. Must have advanced skills in breaching demolitions. Applicant should be at least eighteen years old and be very familiar with static line and freefall parachuting as well as scuba diving.

Would you be interested in this job? Would you be willing to learn all the skills it takes to fill a position such as this? These are the skills required to be a member of the Reconnaissance Battalion Marines.

A Tough Job Description

Being a marine takes a solid combination of physical, mental, and emotional stamina. To be a Reconnaissance Battalion Marine requires even more. To even start the process of becoming Recon Marines, men have to pass a physical fitness test that makes most exercise tests pale in comparison. They go to schools that most people have never heard of, let alone imagined attending. They face enormous risks—willingly— that would make most people run in the opposite direction.

Besides the intense training, how else does the job of a Recon Marine differ from other MOSs, or military occupation specialties? In the past, Recon Marines were paid no more than other marines, although they were given hazard pay if they had to do extra high-risk work. This changed in 2007, however, when a $61,000 bonus was offered to encourage more marines to go into recon.

The Recon Marines are not only at the front of every mission but are way ahead. They go all the way past enemy lines, sent in ahead of everyone else to get top-secret, essential information about an enemy situation

To jump out of a helicopter and use a parachute, you must know how to land. Marines practice the technique at Camp LeJeune, North Carolina, in the early morning hours.

and to report back to higher command. They are the foot patrols who bravely trespass into extremely unfriendly territory, even though the punishment for getting caught may well be their lives.

Accepting the Mission

The official mission of Recon Marines is complex and can help one understand how serious the job is. The mission includes:

1. Planning, coordinating, and conducting amphibious and ground reconnaissance where they are to watch, identify, and report all enemy activity, plus collect additional data that superiors might find helpful.
2. Conducting terrain reconnaissance that includes hydrography, beaches, roads, bridges, routes, urban areas, helicopter landing zones, airborne drop zones, aircraft forward operating sites, and mounted reconnaissance missions.
3. Organizing with other forces/equipment/personnel, and helping with any engineer, radio, mobile, or other recon missions.
4. Infiltrating mission areas by any means possible, including surface, subsurface, and airborne methods.
5. Conducting counter-reconnaissance.
6. Conducting initial terminal guidance (landing and take-off assistance) for helicopters, landing craft, parachutists, air delivery, and resupply.
7. Designating and/or engaging certain targets with weapons, force fires, and precision-guided munitions to help support others' missions.
8. Conducting post-strike reconnaissance to determine and report battle damages in a specific area.
9. Conducting limited-scale raids and ambushes on targets.

A Marines Corps regiment patrols a rear alley in Ramadi, Iraq, in the photograph above.

What does it take to survive and thrive in such a demanding position as this one? In a Marine Corps article posted on About.com, Staff Sergeant Anthony J. Rivera, a trainer in the 1st Reconnaissance Battalion, says, "To be successful, you can't just say it takes one type of person. You just got to have heart. You just have to have that desire."

Accepting the Creed

Another way to understand the dedication that goes into being a Reconnaissance Marine is to read through the Recon Creed.

The Recon Battalion Marines' Creed

The Recon Battalion Marines' Creed focuses the group's mission into three simple but definitive words. In Latin, the creed is *Celer, Silens, Mortalis*. This translates to "Swift, Silent, Deadly."

Each letter in "recon" stands for an important value. For example, the "R" stands for "Realizing it is my choice and my choice alone to be a Reconnaissance Marine." By accepting the position, the marine also must accept all of the challenges that come with it and promise to do so with honor so as to "maintain the tremendous reputation of those who went before . . . "

The "E" represents "Exceeding beyond the limitations set down by others." This involves sacrificing personal wants and needs, thereby dedicating oneself to being in recon, including maintaining a high level of physical fitness, a positive mental attitude, and high ethics.

The "C" in "recon" stands for "Conquering all obstacles" and a marine's responsibility to endure and never, ever quit. To a Recon Marine, quitting is the same as failing. Instead, he must be able to "overcome, to adapt and to do whatever it takes to complete the mission."

The "O" represents being "On the battlefield," where a Recon Marine should behave with pride and integrity, becoming a person that other marines can emulate.

Finally, the "N" stands for "Never forgetting the principles of a Recon Marine": "Honor, Perseverance, Spirit and Heart."

As Recon Marines will proudly tell you, they "can speak without saying a word and achieve what others can only imagine." But perhaps the best summation of what they are all about was given by 1st Sergeant Erik Shirreffs of the First Reconnaissance Battalion in a Marine Corps News Service article posted on About.com: "Reconnaissance Marines have a reputation as the best of the best. We bring the finest the Marine Corps have to offer."

Recon Marines sometimes make the ultimate sacrifice. Cpl. Paul King, age twenty-three, of Tyngsboro, Massachusetts, was killed June 25, 2006, in Iraq during combat operations.

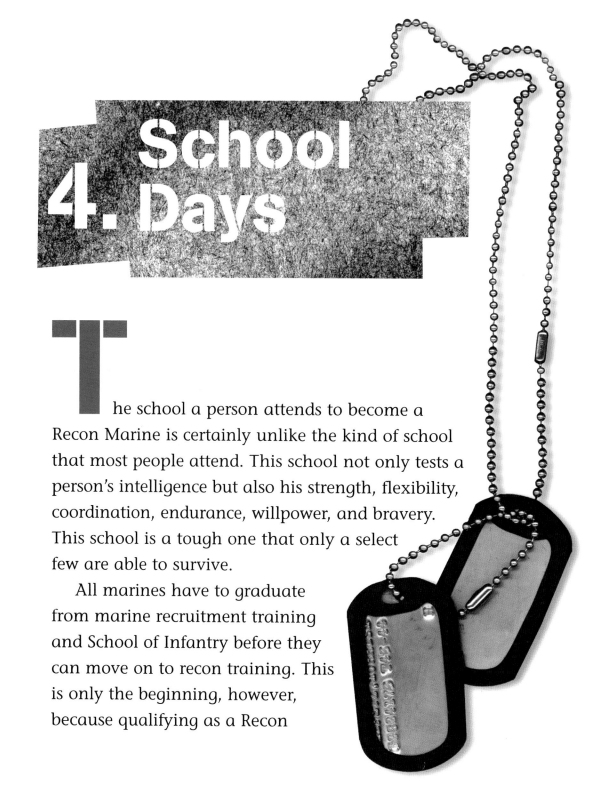

4. School Days

The school a person attends to become a Recon Marine is certainly unlike the kind of school that most people attend. This school not only tests a person's intelligence but also his strength, flexibility, coordination, endurance, willpower, and bravery. This school is a tough one that only a select few are able to survive.

All marines have to graduate from marine recruitment training and School of Infantry before they can move on to recon training. This is only the beginning, however, because qualifying as a Recon

Marine involves a rigorous screening process. The physical fitness test involves a 3-mile (5 km) run (one hundred points for completion in eighteen minutes or less); twenty dead-hang pull-ups (one hundred points for completing all twenty); thirty sit-ups (one hundred points if completed in under two minutes); two obstacle courses (each one completed in under two hours); a 1,640-foot (500 meters) swim in full clothing (completed in seventeen minutes or less); and a 10-mile (16 km) run wearing a 50-pound (23 kilograms) pack (completed in under two hours).

To further determine his fitness level, a marine may be tested to see how many push-ups, flutter kicks, or scissor kicks he can do in two minutes. For those who hope to make it into recon training, a total of 275 is required for enlisted men and 285 for officers. Additional fitness tests include a deep-water rifle retrieval, a tower jump, a thirty-minute water tread, and a five-minute flotation with inflated trousers.

In addition to passing these physical fitness tests, a Recon Marine must have at least 20/20 vision, be a U.S. citizen, be fluent in English, and be a volunteer in the Marine Corps.

Welcome to SERE

After the above requirements are met, the next step is SERE, otherwise known as Survival, Evasion, Resistance, and Escape

During training, marines learn close-quarter combat skills, such as the correct way to handle a detainee, as shown in this photo.

school. The training curriculum at SERE is divided into three parts. The first one is Survival and Evasion. This is the main focus of the school. The skills taught in this portion of the course include wilderness survival (including a wide range of natural climates), emergency first aid, land navigation, camouflage techniques, evasion techniques, communication protocols, and construction of improvised tools. More skills are taught, but they are considered classified by the U.S. government and thus cannot be disclosed to the public.

The second portion is Resistance and Escape. This focuses on how to cope if one falls into the hands of the enemy. The lessons are based on the real-life experiences of formerly captured Americans. While much of this section is classified as secret by the U.S.

government, some basic information is known. As might be guessed from its name, the training is not easy or enjoyable. Its aim is to be as realistic as possible. It shows marines how to handle imprisonment, torture, and brainwashing. It provides a completely authentic simulation of the cruel and abusive coercive techniques that captors often use and how to effectively resist them.

Water survival is another type of recon training. Cpl. Jeffrey Baker of the 3rd Reconnaissance Battalion, 3rd Marine Division drifts in the Pacific Ocean after a 2,000-meter open swim.

The last portion of the training curriculum is Water Survival. It centers on teaching the skills needed to survive situations in an aquatic environment. It is brief, lasting only two days, during which marines are taught emergency first aid tailored to the aquatic environment, communication protocols, ocean ecology, equipment maintenance, and the handling of aquatic survival gear.

One Shot, One Kill

Scanning the horizon for any possible Iraqi insurgents is Staff Sergeant Timothy LaSage, a sniper with the 2nd Battalion, 5th Marine Regiment.

Another class that Recon Marines attend if they are pursuing a combat arms specialty is a ten-week course at sniper school. "The Marine Corps has the best sniper program in the world," says Gunnery Sergeant Richard Tisdale in the article "Marine Corps Sniper Training," posted online at the Marine Corps News Service. "A sniper needs to be trained as best as possible because they must be combat ready at all times. Due to the nature of the sniper's mission, they must be trained mentally and physically to operate independently forward of friendly positions on the battlefield."

The sniper school includes courses on land navigation, field sketches, range estimations, marksmanship, surveillance, academics, and stalking. Sergeant Dain K. Doughty, a graduate of sniper school, says on Leatherneck.com, "In the stalking portion, you have three hours to move within 200 meters [656 feet] of two highly trained observers and set up a shooting position. These guys can spot a leaf turned upside down from a mile away, so you've really got to focus on blending in with your environment."

Tisdale notes in the Leatherneck.com article, "We train our snipers to be patient and wait for the perfect opportunity to fire upon the target when it will best support the mission. They could lie in a dormant position for days at a time before actually pulling the trigger and engaging on the target."

School of Stress

One of the most challenging schools that a Recon Marine may enroll in is the U.S. Army Ranger School. This nine-week course takes place in three different locations: Fort Benning, Georgia (for the woodland terrain portion); Camp Rogers, Camp Darby, and Camp Merrill in Georgia; and Camp Rudder in Florida. Each session lasts for three weeks.

What makes this course so intense and powerful is that the students are put through experiences as uncomfortable, stressful, and fatiguing as those that marines may have to

Here, a U.S. Army Ranger shows the proper way to drop from a rope forty feet into a pond below. Since a ranger's main job is to engage in close combat, he has to be ready to infiltrate areas in many ways.

cope with on a real mission. Scenarios are set up where students have to move into "enemy" territory, including the rough terrain around Fort Benning, the mountains of Georgia, and the swamps and coastlines of Florida.

Throughout the course of the day, the students carry gear weighing 100 pounds (45 kg) or more as they go on patrols, participate in ambushes and raids against targets, or conduct reconnaissance. Training often runs as long as twenty hours per day, and the men average less than four hours of sleep each night. Some nights they may get more, but on others, they may get none at all. They are fed only once or twice a day, resulting in overwhelming mental and physical fatigue and stress.

The first phase of the training, which is at Fort Benning, is referred to as the "crawl" phase. It includes a physical fitness test that requires forty-nine-plus push-ups, fifty-nine-plus sit-ups, six chin-ups, and a 5-mile (8 km) individual run in uniform and running shoes (in forty minutes or less). Other activities at Fort Benning include:

- A combat water survival assessment and water confidence test.
- A combination night/day land navigation test.
- Modern Army Combative Program training each night for several hours in sawdust pits.
- A 1.63-mile (2.6 km) terrain run followed by an obstacle course that includes the infamous "worm pit," a shallow, muddy, 82-foot (25 m) obstacle course covered by knee-high barbed wire. It has to be completed more than once—on back and belly.
- Demolitions training and airborne refresher training.
- A 12-mile (19 km) individual march that must be completed in three hours and fifteen minutes or less.

In the next phase, marines are instructed in squad combat operations. Training includes more obstacle courses as well as patrolling drills and battle drills designed to replicate contact with the enemy, breaking contact, enemy ambushes, and platoon raids. Finally, the students learn about the roles of both leading and supporting through a series of student-led tactical operations.

Paying a Price

How does the Ranger course affect the average marine's body?
Typical weight loss is between 35 pounds (16 kg) and 50 pounds
(23 kg). While men are enrolled in the Ranger School, they must
constantly deal with on-and-off rushes of stress hormones, which
is hard on the body. The lack of sleep and constant physical
demands can take a serious toll on students, sometimes resulting
in dehydration, heatstroke, frostbite, muscle injuries, severe cuts,
and even potentially lethal bites from insects, scorpions, or snakes.

The next phase in the Ranger School is the mountain
phase. Here, marines learn all about military mountaineering
skills amid rugged terrain, severe weather, constant hunger,
extreme fatigue, and severe emotional stress. Knowledge
imparted during this phase includes information about knots,
belays, anchor points, rope management, and the fundamentals
of climbing and rappelling. All of these lessons are then tested
with a conflict scenario set in the mountains. It takes place
night and day for a total of eight days and involves cross-
country patrolling, coping with vehicle ambushes, attacking

mortar and communication sites, conducting a river crossing, and climbing a steep mountainside. Though most likely exhausted, hungry, short-tempered, and frustrated, any one of the students may be asked to lead the others in any part of the combat mission.

On this course, marines practice rope climbing. This requires a great deal of arm strength and endurance, both of which will come in handy when they are out in the field.

The third and final phase of the training takes place in Florida's Camp Rudder. Here, the terrain consists of steamy, hot, and humid swamps and forests. The focus shifts to small-boat operations, stream-crossing techniques, and other aspects of survival required in this wet environment.

Grading performances at Ranger School begins with an evaluation of each person's overall leadership abilities during the course. Each marine is given a "Go" or a "No Go." Another part of the grading process is peer evaluation. What a student's peers think of him is very important in this kind of training.

Ready, Set, Dive!

Yet another type of school Recon Marines can participate in is the thirty-five-day Marine Corps Combatant Diver Course (MCCDC). It is designed to prepare the men physically and mentally through a combination of extremely rigorous physical exercise and classroom lessons on the basics of dive medicine, dive tables, and dive principles. Students participate in running and water aerobic exercises, followed by open-water swimming with fins. While these marines swim, they also must wear heavy vests and simulated guns and ammunition.

"By the end of the course, they will be swimming 2,000 yards [1,829 m] in open water," says Gunnery Sergeant Mark Altenburg, the training chief for Headquarters and Service Company, 3rd Reconnaissance Battalion, on the Web site of the Okinawa, Japan, Marine Corps base. "They need to be ready for the MCCDC. By the time they complete that course, they will have finned 63,000 yards [57,607 m]—roughly thirty-seven miles [60 km]. We are trying to set them up for success." Altenburg further states, "The MCCDC is extremely demanding, both physically and mentally. We want to send them to the dive course with a good understanding of the academic portion of the course, as well as being strong swimmers."

Other schools that Recon Marines can go to include Military Free Fall School and Helicopter Rope Suspension Training. In the

Free Fall School, marines are taught a new way of parachuting out of an airplane. In the traditional type of jump, the marine falls straight down and both he and the plane can be easily detected by the enemy. With this new type of parachute (known as an SF-10A), people can jump from 13,000 feet (3,962 m) in elevation or even as high as 20,000 feet (6,096 m). This results in the parachute opening much higher up, so the sound of it cannot be heard and tracked from the ground by the enemy.

High-altitude parachuting allows marines to slip into enemy territory unseen and unheard. With oxygen and all of the combat equipment on their backs, they land ready to go right into battle.

Instead of falling straight down, the jumper can steer the parachute for several miles, allowing him to exit the plane even farther from the enemy site and thus making it much harder to detect the jumper or the plane from which he jumped. On Global Security.org, Captain Jonathan R. Smith, a

Reconnaissance and Survival platoon commander, says, "With this type of insertion, the enemy will never hear you. You could fly in [at a high altitude] over an anti-aircraft or radar threat and make a final foot movement to the objective." Primary jumpmaster Sergeant Todd Smalenberg adds, "Every time we roll out of the camp in vehicles, the enemy knows. I feel safer doing this than driving my vehicle out of the camp. This is the best means [of insertion]. Besides, it's just another way to get to work."

Learning how to jump properly and safely with this new kind of parachute entails extra training. When preparing to make that leap out of the helicopter or plane, marines have a lot to keep in mind. "It's important to remember to make sure you have a tight body position and to know what to do if, when you jump, you get a partial or total malfunction of the parachute," explains Recon Marine corporal Jeffrey Elmore, in an article for the Marine Corps News Web site. "After jumping out, we have to keep our feet and knees together to avoid injuries such as broken legs upon landing," adds Corporal Robertson Greenbacker. "We also need to tuck our chins to our chest or else whiplash could occur."

Training for the SF-10A typically takes days with multiple jumps, with and without gear. Night jumps are also part of the training. The trainers carry a great deal of responsibility, too. "We keep in constant contact with the Marines on the

Being the First

It isn't easy being the first one to jump out of a helicopter, even if you are a marine. "As the first Marine to jump out," admits Corporal Michael Figueroa, "I stood there at the back edge of the helicopter and just said, 'Whoa.' After we got the go ahead to jump, the feeling pretty much changed to a 'let's do it' attitude. It's harder to be the first jumper." He adds, "When you're behind people, it's just a matter of following and watching the person in front of you."

ground to ensure the drop zone is ready for the jump," explained Sergeant Eric Guevara, crew chief. "The jumpmasters aboard the aircraft get the go-ahead from the pilot and, in turn, tell the jumpers when to go. After those Marines jump, it is our responsibility to keep track of them until they land."

In short, going to school has a much different meaning for the Recon Marine. It means less reading and more rappelling, less math and more maneuvering, less science and more swimming, and unending endurance and determination. Academics aside, it takes a commitment to your country, a belief in yourself, and a dedication to the armed forces to be a Recon Marine.

5. The Tools and Equipment

Have you ever had to do a job that required specialized tools or equipment? No matter how dedicated you might be to that job, completing it will be more than challenging if you don't have the necessary supplies. It is much the same with Recon Marines. Some of the missions they go on may require little more than stealth, skill, knowledge, and bravery, but others may require specialized tools and equipment that are the keys to success.

Body Wear

One of the most important pieces of clothing that a Recon Marine wears is a Full Spectrum Battle Equipment Amphibious Assault Vest Quick Release, or FSBE AAV QR for short. This lightweight vest does two essential things. First, it gives protection. It has soft armor built in, plus hard ballistic inserts, or plates that help stop bullets from hitting the skin. One is made to protect the throat and another protects the groin. In addition to providing protection, this vest also has multiple pockets and pouches for carrying whatever you might need while out in the field.

A marine with the 3rd Platoon, Bravo Company, 3rd Reconnaissance Battalion looks carefully through the site of his gun during a January 2007 patrol in Rutbah, Iraq.

One of the best features of this specially made vest is its quick release, or "ditch," ability. It is made to come off quickly so that a marine can leave it behind in case of an emergency. This feature was developed for a good reason. In December 1999, several members of a unit were in a helicopter crash over the Pacific Ocean and unfortunately drowned because they were not able to shed their vests fast enough to swim away from the wreckage. Only one marine survived the accident.

Another piece of body armor given to Recon Marines is the Modular Integrated Communications Helmet, or MICH. This helmet has the ability to do multiple things at once: it protects the marine's head and at the same time is a communications tool. It has a built-in headset and microphone for keeping in touch with other marines as well as superiors.

Most marines will also wear a new type of uniform called the MARPAT, or Marine Disruptive Pattern uniform. The camouflage pattern on it is created by tiny, rectangular pixels of color that imitate the dappled textures and abstract boundaries found in the wild. This new technique of creating a pattern helps to make a marine even more invisible when he goes on a mission. These uniforms are often referred to as "digi-cammies" and are produced in two styles: woodland and desert.

Weaponry

One of the weapons that's commonly used by Recon Marines is the MEU (SOC) pistol. Each one is hand-built from parts from different manufacturers, so no two are exactly alike.

They are assembled by specially trained employees of the Rifle Team Equipment Shop, Quantico, Virginia. The MEU (SOC) is considered to be one of the most reliable weapons on the market but is in the midst of being replaced by an improved version. Other common weapons used by Recon Marines include:

- M4A1 close-quarters battle weapons
- M2093 grenade launchers
- M40 sniper rifles
- M14 designated marksmen rifles
- M249 squad automatic weapons
- M240 general purpose machine guns
- M2HB heavy machine guns

Accuracy with weapons is one of the biggest requirements for becoming a member of the Reconnaissance Battalions. Marines spend many hours practicing in order to meet their pistol qualifications.

For the Terrain

Getting from one place to another quickly and safely is an important part of any mission, including reconnaissance. The Recon Marines have several options. One is the Interim Fast Attack Vehicle. Previously, desert patrol vehicles were used, but they did not have enough firepower, nor were they big enough to carry everything the marines wanted. The Fast Attack was the replacement.

Another vehicle used is the LAV-25, which stands for "light armored vehicle." This all-terrain, all-weather vehicle can travel as well in the nighttime as it does in the daytime. It can be transported from one place to another by air, and with only a three-minute warning, it can change from a land to a water vehicle, complete with two propellers and four rudders. Top speed on the ground is 62 miles per hour (100 kilometers per hour), while top speed in the water is 6 miles per hour (10 km per hour). Typical weaponry includes a chain gun, two machine guns, and smoke grenades. It usually holds three people: the driver, the gunner, and the vehicle commander.

For underwater approaches, some Recon Marines ride in a small vehicle called the Diver Propulsion Device (DPD). It is able to transport two marines underwater to a set destination, getting them onto a beach without their having to swim a long distance or be seen. "It greatly minimizes the physical impact on the Marines," says Senior Chief Petty Officer Christopher Weaver, a master diver, in an article for the Marine Corps News Web site. "If they have to do an insertion, they don't have to fin for 10,000 yards [9,144 m]. They can use the DPD and drive in; that way they have more energy and more reserves to focus on the mission once they're on the beach." The DPD has depth gauges, an

Some Reconnaissance Battalion members spend many hours in and under the water, as well as on the ground and in the air. Training with the Diver Propulsion Device takes time and skill.

onboard compass, and rechargeable batteries; plus it is strong enough to withstand rough waters and strong currents. "A swimmer may be able to go against a one-knot current but not much more," adds Weaver. "The DPD allows us to swim against much greater currents. We can go in and out [from the shore] without the current being too much of a factor."

Learning to use the DPD takes extra training, of course, and most Recon Marines are taught in a one-week course. They go to classes, take tests, and finally get in the water and do hands-on work with the machine itself. "It is important to train on [the DPD] now," says Sergeant Nicholas Koumalatsos,

Hoping for a Hybrid

An old radio show told listeners that "only the Shadow knows." In this case, the Shadow was an invincible crime fighter. But when it comes to Recon Marines, the Shadow is an RST-V, or Reconnaissance, Surveillance, and Targeting Vehicle. It is the newest vehicle made for use on recon missions. It has a hybrid electric and diesel drive, so it is both fast and quiet. It is able to reach 70 miles per hour (113 km per hour) and has four-by-four capabilities for cross-country travel. It can run on batteries alone for approximately 20 miles (32 km) and can easily be transported by helicopter. Recon units will use it for many things, including fire-support coordination, forward air control (directing aircraft from the ground), reconnaissance, light strikes, and anti-armor or air defense. The vehicle can also serve as everything from a battlefield ambulance to a cargo or personnel carrier to a mortar carrier to a command post carrier to a mobile, sixty-watt generator.

a Recon Marine, on the Marine Corps News Web site. "If you need to use one in an actual mission and you've never used it before—it's too late. During the mission is not the time to learn." As one master gunnery sergeant puts it, "It's just another tool in the Recon shed."

Going on the Greenside

What equipment a unit uses depends largely on its mission and location. Greenside operations, for example, are those that are not intended to include any face-to-face or direct contact with enemy forces. Most recon missions tend to be of this type. Since they are often far ahead of the rest of the force, Recon Marines rely heavily on their ability to be quiet and invisible. Typically, a Greenside recon mission marine would carry:

- A "boonie hat," which looks much like a fisherman's hat with a camouflage pattern on it.
- A camouflage utility uniform: These uniforms have a digital or pixilated camouflage pattern on them.
- A load-bearing vest for protection as well as for carrying ammunition and supplies.
- A rucksack or large backpack for carrying the items that do not need to be accessed often.
- Rations, including toiletries, fuel, water, etc.
- Primary weapon.
- A sidearm (occasionally).

Other armor is not usually used in Greenside missions because it is heavy, hot, and noisy.

Going to the Blackside

Direct-action operations are also referred to as Blackside operations. They include a strong chance that the Recon Marines will come into close, personal contact with the enemy. The recovery of aircraft personnel, raids on gas or oil platforms, and search and seizures are all examples of this kind of mission. On Blackside operations, Recon Marines may be accompanied by specialists, such as experts in removing and disarming explosives. They may reach their mission sites by foot, vehicle, parachute, helicopter, or water. Typically, these marines carry:

- A MICH helmet.
- A hands-free communications headset.
- Tactical goggles.
- A NOMEX (fire-retardant fabric) balaclava (hood with a large opening for the eyes).
- A NOMEX flight suit.
- NOMEX aviator gloves in sage green or khaki.
- A vest with attached pouches to hold everything from ammunition, grenades, and breaching charges to gas masks, medical supplies, and communications equipment. (Armor, in the form of ballistic insert plates, is included in the vest.)

- A pistol belt or rigger's belt with suspenders to carry pouches or other devices.
- A thigh-mounted tactical holster to hold the MEU (SOC) and sidearm. Sometimes a flashlight is installed under the frame.
- A holster on the opposite leg of the marine's dominant hand for stowing ammunition.
- Knee pads and elbow pads, both for shielding and to protect the marine's joints from the stress and discomfort of various firing or waiting positions.
- A close-quarters battle weapon, often accompanied by reflex sights and attachments.
- Boots or specialized hiking shoes.

To ensure his safety and effectiveness, a marine must be well equipped. Some staples include the MICH helmet, communications headset, and tactical goggles.

Having the right equipment when on a mission is vital. It makes a tough job a little easier and a lot safer. When it comes to being a Recon Marine, anything that can make the job safer is a good thing for the marines—and for the country.

Glossary

amphibious Able to live on land and in water.

aquatic Taking place or practiced on or in the water.

artillery Mounted guns or missile launchers; may be either mobile or stationary.

ballistic Of or relating to the study of projectiles, especially as related to firearms.

camouflage Clothing made of fabric with a mottled design, usually in shades of green and brown; to disguise, hide, or deceive.

civilian A person who is not on active duty with a military, naval, police, or firefighting organization.

covert Concealed, secret, or disguised.

dehydration An abnormal loss of water from the body or from an organ or body part, as from illness or fluid deprivation.

dormant In a state of rest or inactivity; inoperative.

enlisted A military rank below a commissioned officer or warrant officer.

insurgent A person who rises in forcible opposition to lawful authority, especially a person who engages in armed resistance to a government or to the execution of its laws.

intelligence information Important details about an enemy or a potential enemy.

motto A brief statement used to express a principle, goal, or ideal.

rappel To lower oneself from a height by means of a double rope secured from above, placed around the body, and paid out gradually in the descent.

reconnaissance A search made for useful military information in the field.

recruit To engage persons for military service.

ruck A slang term for a rucksack or backpack.

stealth Conducting secret, clandestine, or surreptitious procedures.

surveillance A watch kept over a person, suspect, or prisoner.

For More Information

Marine Corps Community Services

3280 Russell Road

Quantico, VA 22134

Web site: http://www.usmc-mccs.org

Marine Corps Community Services offers services to aid marines and their families. The Web site contains information on operations and responses to recent media queries that will give a perspective on how benefits are provided for marines and their families.

Marine Corps/Sniper Association

P.O. Box 762

Quantico, VA 22134

(877) 635-1775

Web site: http://www.usmcscoutsniper.org/association.htm

The home page of the USMC Scout/Sniper Association has up-to-date news about the actions of marines around the world.

U.S. Marines Corps Headquarters

2008 Elliot Road

Quantico, VA 22134

Web site: http://www.usmc.mil/marinelink/mcn2000.nsf/
    homepage?readform

The official homepage of the U.S. Marine Corps provides information for interested recruits, as well as news, history, and other information.

Web Sites

Due to the changing nature of Internet links, Rosen Publishing has developed an online list of Web sites related to the subject of this book. This site is updated regularly. Please use this link to access the list:

http://www.rosenlinks.com/iso/urba

For Further Reading

Aaseng, Nathan. *The Marine Corps in Action*. Berkeley Heights, NJ: Enslow Publishers, 2001.

Benson, Michael. *The U.S. Marine Corps*. Minneapolis, MN: Lerner Publications, 2004.

Cureton, Charles. *The U.S. Marines Corps: The Illustrated History of the American Soldier, His Uniform and His Equipment*. New York, NY: Chelsea House Publications, 1999.

Doeden, Matt, and Barbara Fox. *The U.S Marine Corps*. Mankato, MN: Capstone Press, 2005.

Hamilton, John. *The Marine Corps*. Edina, MN: Checkerboard Books, 2007.

Payment, Simone. *Frontline Marines: Fighting in the Marine Combat Arms Unit*. New York, NY: Rosen Publishing Group, 2007.

Voeller, Edward. *U.S. Marine Corps Special Forces: Recon Marines*. Mankato, MN: Capstone Press, 2000.

Bibliography

About.com. "Marine Corps Recon Screening." October 4, 2003. Retrieved November 26, 2007 (http://usmilitary.about.com/cs/marines/a/reconselection.htm).

About.com. "Marine Corps Scout Sniper Training." September 3, 2003. Retrieved November 26, 2007 (http://usmilitary.about.com/cs/marines/a/marinesniper.htm).

Blodgett, Lance Corporal Corey. "Recon Marines Get In-depth Training." Marine Corps News, August 24, 2007. Retrieved November 26, 2007 (http://www.usmc.mil/marinelink/mcn2000.nsf/main5/90A9F6904122266985257341001AFD9C?opendocument).

Bradley, Gunnery Sergeant Mark. "Recon Makes Transition." GlobalSecurity.org. Retrieved November 26, 2007 (http://www.globalsecurity.org/military/library/news/2003/02/mil-030225-usmc02.htm).

Crawford, Lance Corporal Kimberly. "HMH-461 Lets Marines Leap from 'Perfectly Good Aircraft.'" Marine Corps News, April 12, 2007. Retrieved November 28, 2007 (http://www. usmc.mil/marinelink/mcn2000.nsf/ac95bc775efc34c685256 ab50049d458/7c49f27c3365d7a0852572c100577aee? OpenDocument).

Johnston, Lance Corporal Adam. "MP Earns Medal for Graduation Scout Sniper School with Top Honors." Leatherneck.com, May 5, 2006. Retrieved November 26, 2007 (http://www.leatherneck.com/forums/showthread. php?t=29505).

Joy, Elizabeth. "The Meaning of Oorah Traced Back to Its Roots." Flickr, October 8, 2004. Retrieved November 26, 2007 (http:// www.flickr.com/groups/semperfi/discuss/72157603174221773).

Military.com. "Recon Marines Destroy Terrorist Cell." October 8, 2007. Retrieved November 26, 2007 (http://www.military.com/ features/0,15240,151960,00.html?ESRC=marine.nl).

Oliva, Gunnery Sergeant Mark. "Marine Recon Adapts to Growing Mission in Iraq." Marine Corps News, May 17, 2006. Retrieved November 26, 2007 (http://www.usmc. mil/marinelink/mcn2000.nsf/main5/F0C8CDC3863FCE878 5257176002C022D?opendocument).

Oliva, Gunnery Sergeant Mark. "Second Recon Battalion Marines Keep Insurgents on the Run During Operation Matador." Marine Corps News, September 13, 2006.

Retrieved November 27, 2007 (http://192.156.19.109/
marinelink/mcn2000.nsf/main5/70FD1CB70701186085257
1E9002EA924?opendocument).

Peace, Lance Corporal Warren. "Swift, Silent, Deadly Marines
Prepare for Dive School." U.S. Marines in Japan. December 13,
2005. Retrieved November 26, 2007 (http://www.okinawa.
usmc.mil/Public%20Affairs%20Info/Archive%20News%20P
ages/2005/051213-scuba.html).

Index

About the Author

Tamra Orr is the author of more than one hundred nonfiction books for kids of all ages. She lives in the Pacific Northwest with her husband and children, who range in age from eleven to twenty-three. In her free time, Orr reads voraciously, appreciates the mountains on the horizon, and reflects on all of the things she has learned by writing so many books.

Photo Credits

Cover, cover (inset), pp. 1, 4, 17, 25, 32, 33, 39, 41, 45, 47, 49 U.S. Marine Corps/Department of Defense; pp. 9, 11, 21, 22, 53 © Getty Images; p. 14 © Corbis; pp. 16, 27, 29, 34 © AP Photos; p. 36 © AFP/Getty Images.

Designer: Les Kanturek; **Editor:** Peter Herman
Photo Researcher: Marty Levick